100 Hymns for Flute and Guitar

With Suggested Chordal Accompaniment

By William Bay

WILLIAM BAY **MUSIC**

Distributed by Mel Bay Publications, Inc.

WWW.MELBAY.COM

Index of Hymns

Title	Page

Title	Page

Preface

This is a collection of 100 of my favorite hymns arranged for flute solo. I have written suggested chordal accompaniment for each hymn so that a guitar or any chordal instrument can accompany the solos. Where appropriate, capo chords are shown. I have also indicated whether the guitarist should play fingerstyle or use a strum type accompaniment.

The music in this book spans centuries and represents a wonderful assortment of solos which may be used as preludes or offertories throughout the various seasons in the church year. This series also includes a separate volume for the Christmas season.

These arrangements can add much to any worship service. There is something very captivating about the sound of the flute in worship. I hope these arrangements capture that special sound for you as you play them.

William Bay

A Mighty Fortress is Our God
Ein' Feste Burg

Strum Guitar Acc.

Martin Luther
arr. by William Bay

Boldly ♩ = 90

Abide with Me
Eventide

Fingerstyle Guitar Acc.

William Henry Monk
arr. by William Bay

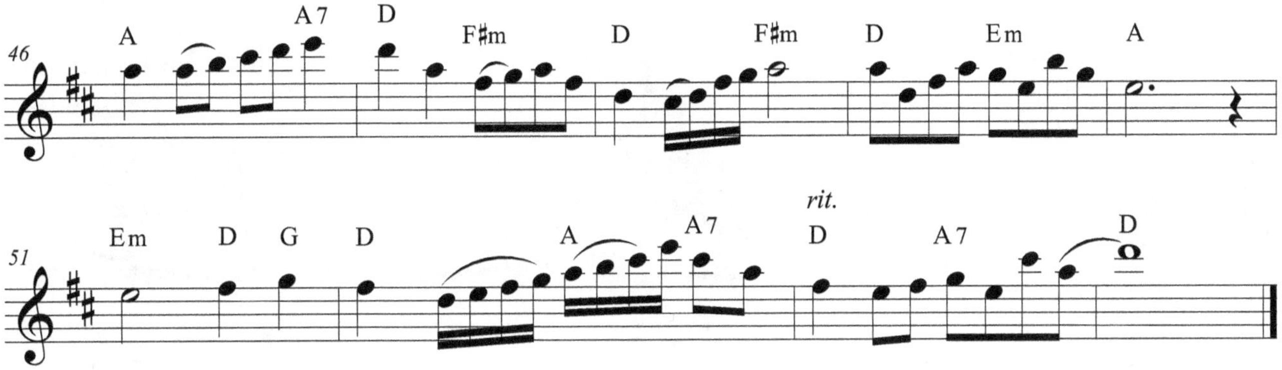
46
A
A7
D
F♯m
D
F♯m
D
Em
A
rit.
51
Em
D
G
D
A
A7
D
A7
D

Adoro Devote

13th Century Plainsong
arr. by William Bay

Ah, Holy Jesus, How Have You Offended
Herzliebster Jesu

Fingerstyle Guitar Acc.

Johann Crüger
arr. by William Bay

Lyrically ♩ = 112

All Creatures of our God and King
Lasst Uns Erfreuen

Strum Guitar Acc.

Majestically ♩ = 94

Giestliche Kirchengesánge
arr. by William Bay

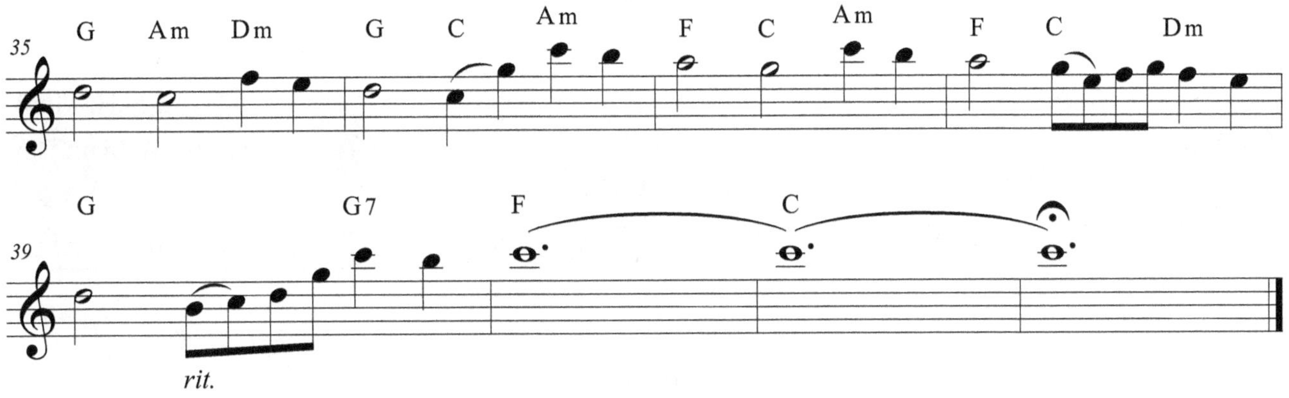
35
G Am Dm G C Am F C Am F C Dm
39
G G7 F C
rit.

All Glory, Laud, and Honor
St. Theodulph

All Hail the Power of Jesus' Name
Coronation

Strum Guitar Acc.

Boldly ♩ = 112

Oliver Holden
arr. by William Bay

All Praise to You, My God This Night
Tallis Canon

Guitar: Capo 3rd Fret and Play Chords in Parentheses

Fingerstyle Guitar Acc.

Thomas Tallis
arr. by William Bay

This page has been left blank to avoid an awkward page turn.

Alleluia! Sing to Jesus
Hyfrydol

Guitar: Capo 3rd Fret and Play Chords in Parentheses

Fingerstyle or Strum Guitar Acc.

Rowland Hugh Prichard
arr. by William Bay

Allegro ♩ = 130

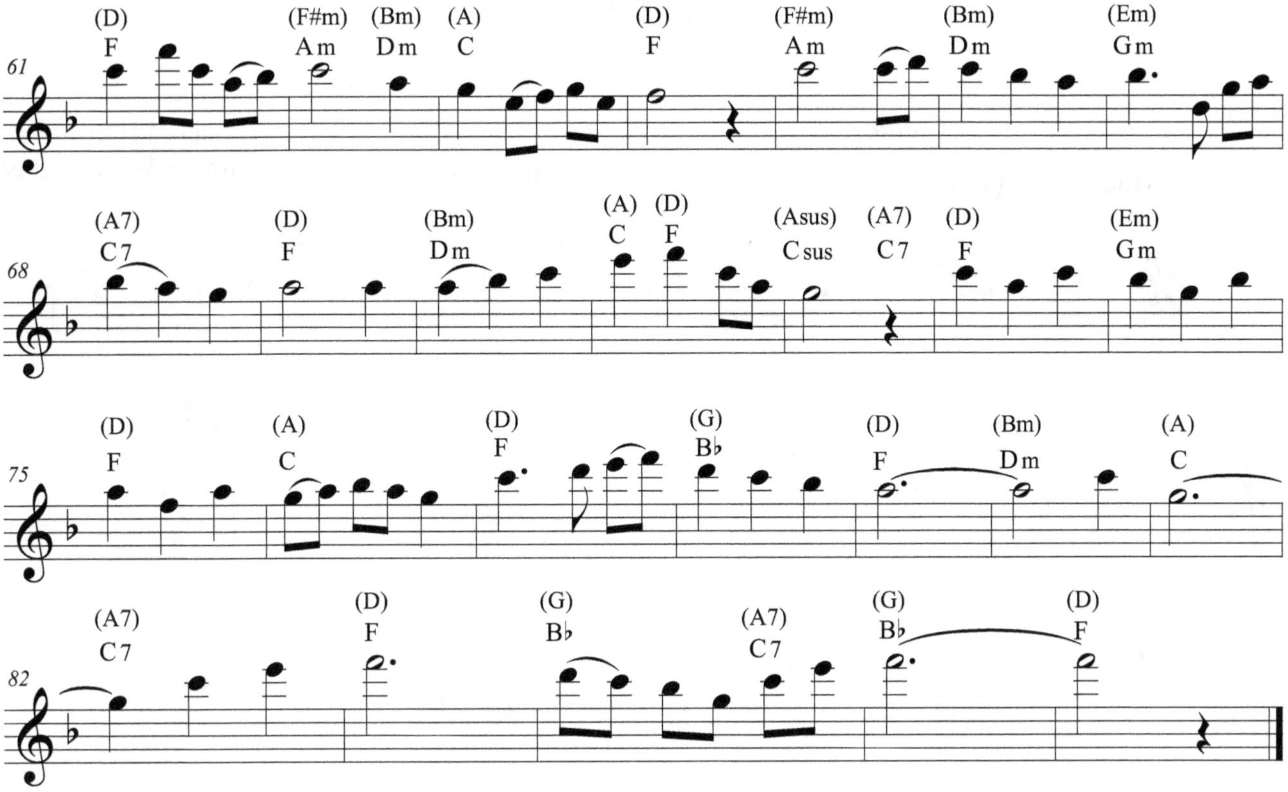
61
(D) F
(F#m) Am
(Bm) Dm
(A) C
(D) F
(F#m) Am
(Bm) Dm
(Em) Gm
68
(A7) C7
(D) F
(Bm) Dm
(A) C
(D) F
(Asus) Csus
(A7) C7
(D) F
(Em) Gm
75
(D) F
(A) C
(D) F
(G) B♭
(D) F
(Bm) Dm
(A) C
82
(A7) C7
(D) F
(G) B♭
(A7) C7
(G) B♭
(D) F

Am I Born to Die?
Idumea

Fingerstyle Guitar Acc.

Sacred Harp, 1835
arr. by William Bay

Moderately (♩=118)

And am I born to die?
To lay this body down?
And must my trembling spirit fly
Into a world unknown!

And Can It Be
Sagina

Strum Guitar Acc.

Thomas Campbell
arr. by William Bay

Joyfully (♩=100)

20

53
Am D G D A7 D G D
59
G D C G D G D7 G
65
D G C A7 D G C
71
D G D G D7 G
rit.
77
C G Am G D7 G

Be Thou My Vision
Slane

Fingerstyle Guitar Acc.

Traditional Irish
arr. by William Bay

Moderately ♩ = 104

Beneath the Cross of Jesus
St. Christopher

Fingerstyle Guitar Acc.

Frederick C. Maker
arr. by William Bay

Moderately ♩ = 96

Bread of the World
Eucharistic Hymn

Fingerstyle Guitar Acc.

John S. B. Hodges, 1868

arr. by William Bay

Gently ♩ = 86

Breathe on Me, Breath of God
Trentham

Fingerstyle Guitar Acc.

Gently (♩ = 96)

Robert Jackson
arr. by William Bay

Christ Be in My Heart
Bi a 'losa im Chroise

Strum or Fingerstyle Guitar Acc.

Traditional Irish
arr. by William Bay

Slowly ♩ = 82

Christ Is Made the Sure Foundation
Westminster Abbey

Strum Guitar Acc.

Henry Purcell
arr. by William Bay

Boldly ♩ = 114

Christ the Lord Has Risen Today
Easter Hymn

Strum Guitar Acc.

Triumphantly ♩ = 106

Lyra Davidica, 1708
arr. by William Bay

Come Ye Faithful, Raise the Strain
St. Kevin

Guitar: Capo 3rd Fret and Play Chords in Parentheses

Arthur S. Sullivan
arr. by William Bay

Fingerstyle or Strum Guitar Acc.

Come Ye Sinners, Poor and Wretched
Beach Spring

Strum or Fingerstyle Guitar Acc.

Sacred Harp, 1835
arr. by William Bay

Moderately ♩ = 88

Come, Christians, Join to Sing
Madrid

Guitar: Capo 3rd Fret and Play Chords in Parentheses

Strum Guitar Acc.

Spanish Melody
arr. by William Bay

Allegro ♩ = 160

Come, Holy Spirit
Abbeville

Fingerstyle Guitar Acc.

Anonymous
From the Sacred Harp

arr. by William Bay

Moderately ♩ = 90

A

Guitar Tacit

B

C

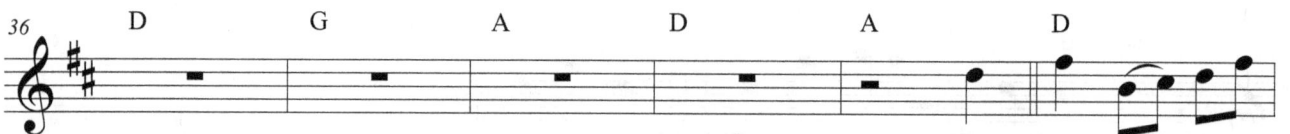

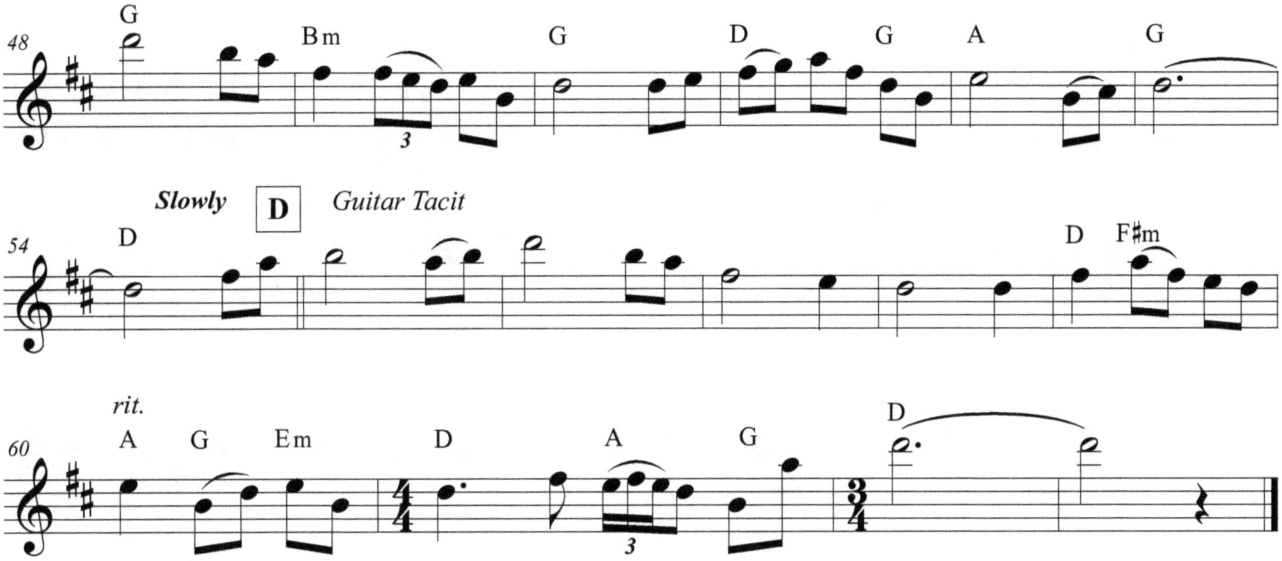
48
G
Bm
G
D
G
A
G
3
Slowly
D
Guitar Tacit
54
D
D
F♯m
rit.
60
A
G
Em
D
A
G
D
3

Come, Thou Fount of Every Blessing
Nettleton

Strum Guitar Acc.

Wyeth's Repository of Sacred Music, 1813

arr. by William Bay

Lively ♩ = 100

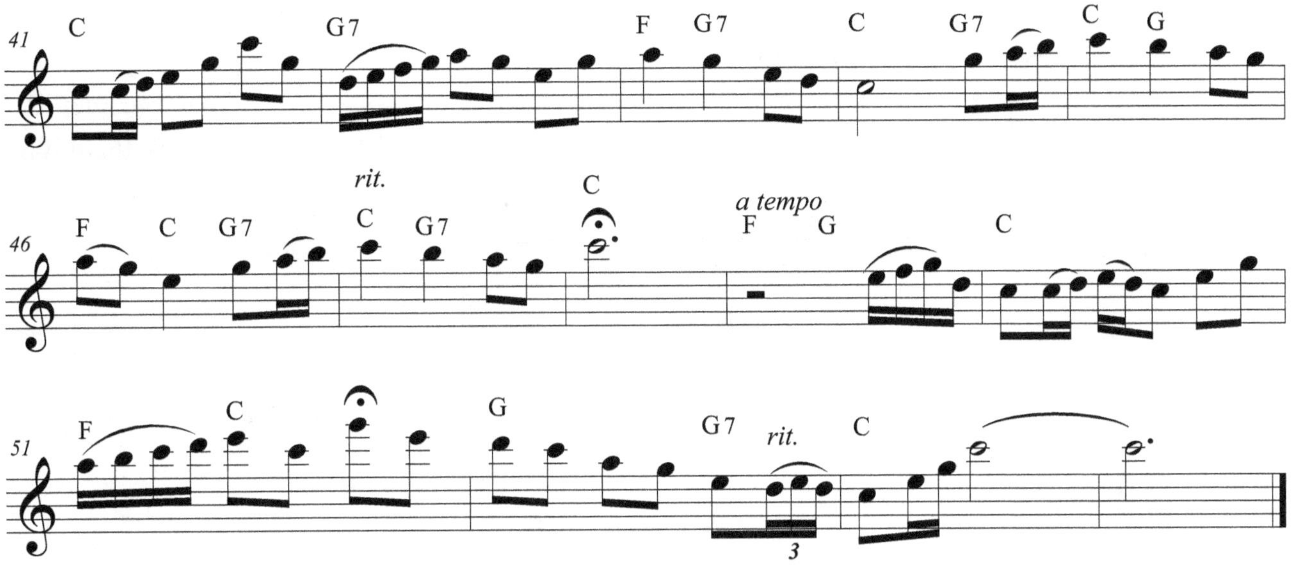
41
C
G7
F G7
C
G7
C G
46
F C G7
rit.
C G7
C
a tempo
F G
C
51
F
C
G
G7
rit.
C
3

Come, Thou Almighty King
Italian Hymn

Fingerstyle or Strum Guitar Acc.

Felice de Giardini
arr. by William Bay

Come, Ye Disconsolate
Consolator

Guitar: Capo 1st Fret and Play Chords in Parentheses

Fingerstyle or Strum Guitar Acc.

Samuel Webbe
arr. by William Bay

Moderato ♩ = 116

Come, Ye Thankful People, Come
St. George's Windsor

Guitar: Capo 3rd Fret and Play Chords in Parentheses

Strum Guitar Acc.

George J. Elvey
arr. by William Bay

Boldly ♩ = 106

Crown Him with Many Crowns
Diademata

Dear Lord and Father of Mankind
Repton

Guitar: Capo 3rd Fret and Play Chords in Parentheses

Fingerstyle Guitar Acc

Charles Hubert Hastings Parry
arr. by William Bay

Moderately ♩ = 96

Doxology
Old 100th

Fingerstyle or Strum Guitar Acc.

Louis Bourgeois
arr. by William Bay

Boldly ♩ = 80

Fairest Lord Jesus
St. Elizabeth

Fingerstyle Guitar Acc.

Lyrically ♩ = 94

Anonymous

arr. by William Bay

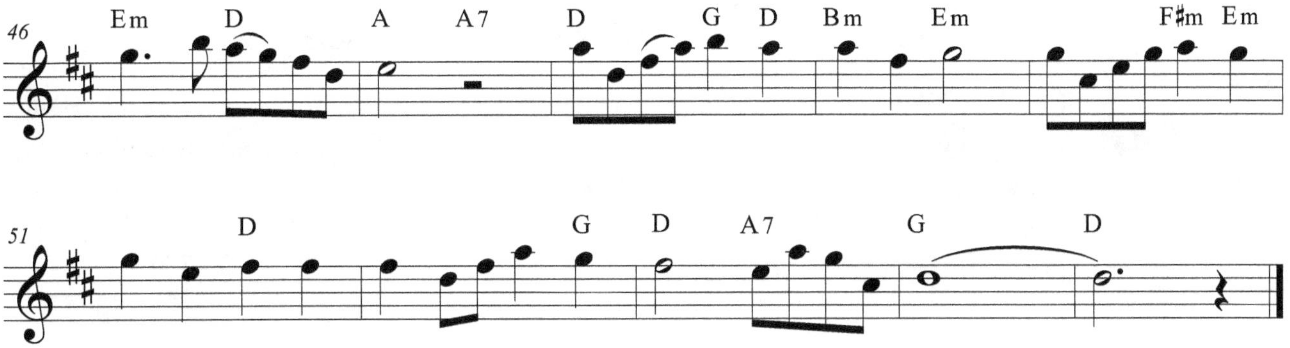
46
Em D A A7 D G D Bm Em F♯m Em
51
D G D A7 G D

Faith of Our Fathers
St. Catherine

Guitar: Capo 3rd Fret and Play Chords in Parentheses

Fingerstyle Guitar Acc.

Henri F. Hemy
arr. by William Bay

Lyrically ♩ = 106

44

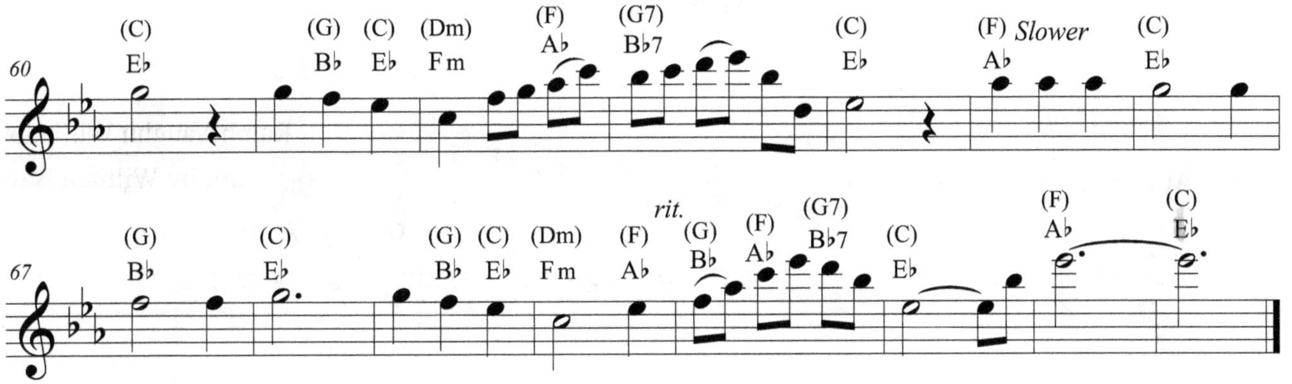
60
(C) E♭
(G) B♭ (C) E♭ (Dm) Fm
(F) A♭ (G7) B♭7
(C) E♭
(F) A♭ Slower
(C) E♭
67
(G) B♭
(C) E♭
(G) B♭ (C) E♭ (Dm) Fm
(F) A♭
rit.
(G) B♭ (F) A♭ (G7) B♭7
(C) E♭
(F) A♭
(C) E♭

For All the Saints
Sine Nomine

Strum Guitar Acc.

Ralph Vaughn Williams
arr. by William Bay

For the Beauty of the Earth
Dix

Fingerstyle Guitar Acc.

Moderato ♩ = 90

Conrad Kocher

arr. by William Bay

Glorious Things of Thee Are Spoken
Austrian Hymn

Strum or Fingerstyle Guitar Acc.

Moderately ♩ = 100

Frans Joseph Haydn

arr. by Wiliam Bay

Glory Be to Jesus
Caswall

Guitar: Capo 3rd Fret and Play Chords in Parentheses

Fingerstyle Guitar Acc.

Friedrich Filitz, 1847
arr. by William Bay

Guide Me, O Thou Great Jehovah
CWM Rhondda

Guitar: Capo 3rd Fret and Play Chords in Parentheses

Strum Guitar Acc.

John Hughes
arr. by William Bay

Hail the Day that Sees Him Rise
Llanfair

Guitar: Capo 3rd Fret and Play Chords in Parentheses

Fingerstyle or Strum Guitar Acc.

Robert Williams
arr. by William Bay

He is Risen
Unser Herrsher

Strum Guitar Acc.

Joachim Neander
arr. by William Bay

Boldly ♩ = 112

Here, O My Lord
Penitentia

Fingerstyle Guitar Acc.

Edward Dearle
arr. by William Bay

Lyrically ♩ = 84

Holy God, We Praise Your Name
Grosser Gott

Fingerstyle Guitar Acc.

Katholisches Gesanbuch

arr. by William Bay

Gently ♩ = 112

Holy, Holy, Holy
Nicaea

Strum Guitar Acc.

John B. Dykes, 1861
arr. by William Bay

Boldly ♩ = 88

Hosanna, Loud Hosanna
Ellacombe

Strum Guitar Acc.

Moderato ♩ = 120

Gesanbuch der Herzogl
arr. by William Bay

This page has been left blank to avoid an awkward page turn

How Sweet the Name of Jesus Sounds
St. Peter

Fingerstyle Guitar Acc.

Alexander R. Reinagle

arr. by William Bay

Moderato ♩ = 98

58

I Love Thy Kingdom, Lord
St. Thomas

Strum Guitar Acc.

Aaron Williams
arr. by William Bay

Moderato ♩ = 116

I Want to Walk as a Child of the Light
Houston

Fingerstyle Guitar Acc.

Kathleen Thomerson
arr. by William Bay

Lyrically ♩ = 106

49 C F Em G C G F C Dm
54 Em C F C F Em Am C Dm C G
D
59 F G C G F Em C F
64 Em C G F C G Am D G
69 Am Em Am Em F G
74 C F Em G rit. C F C

I Will Arise and Go to Jesus
Arise/Restoration

Anonymous
Southern Harmony, 1835
arr. by William Bay

Immortal, Invisible, God Only Wise
St. Denio

Caniadau y Cyssegr
arr. by William Bay

In the Cross of Christ I Glory
Rathbun

Fingerstyle or Strum Guitar Acc.

Ithamar Conkey
arr. by William Bay

64

This page has been left blank to avoid an awkward page turn

It is Well with My Soul
Ville Du Havre

Fingerstyle Guitar Acc.

Philip P. Bliss 1838-1876

arr. by William Bay

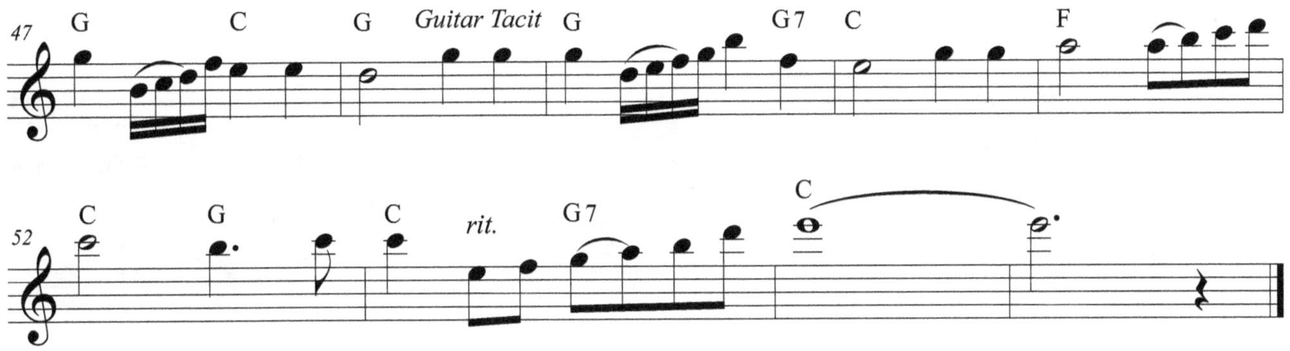
47
G
C
G
Guitar Tacit
G
G7
C
F
52
C
G
C
rit.
G7
C

Jesus Calls Us
Pleading Savior

Fingerstyle or Strum Guitar Acc.

Early American Hymn
arr. by William Bay

Gently ♩ = 84

D
64
D G D A7 D F♯m Bm
72
Em D F♯m Bm F♯m A7 D G D
3
80
A7 D G D Bm A7 D A
88
A7 D G F♯m A D G D
96
Bm A A7 D G D

Jesus Shall Reign
Duke Street

Joyful, Joyful, We Adore Thee
Hymn to Joy

Guitar: Capo 3rd Fret and Play Chords in Parentheses

Ludwig van Beethoven
arr. by William Bay

Strum Guitar Acc.

Boldly ♩ = 114

Land of Rest
Often Sung As "Jerusalem, My Happy Home"

Fingerstyle Guitar Acc.

Early American Melody

arr. by William Bay

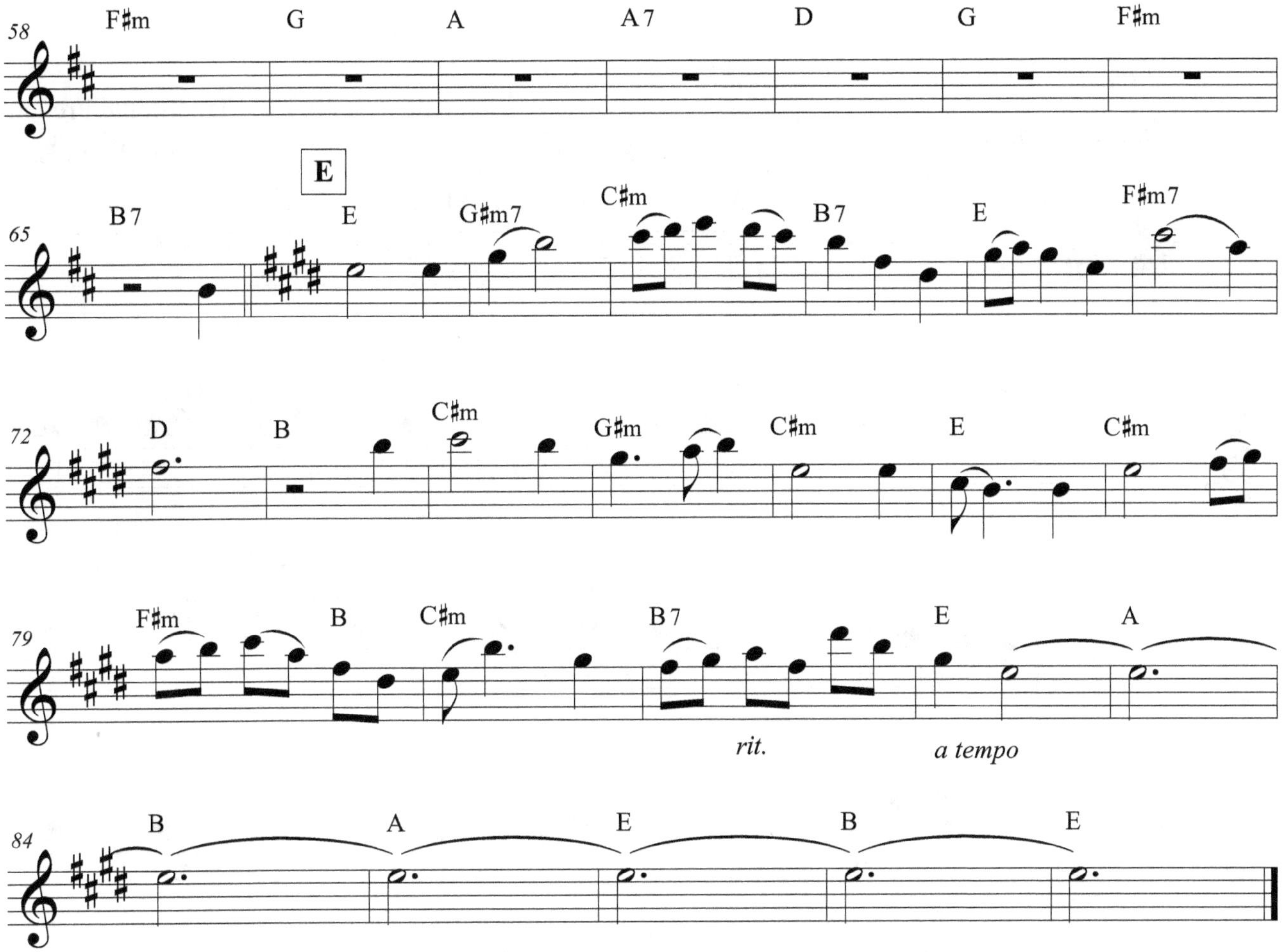
58
F♯m G A A7 D G F♯m
E
65
B7 E G♯m7 C♯m B7 E F♯m7
72
D B C♯m G♯m C♯m E C♯m
79
F♯m B C♯m B7 E A
rit.
a tempo
84
B A E B E

Let All Mortal Flesh Keep Silence
Picardy

Fingerstyle Guitar Acc.

Traditional French
arr. by William Bay

Gently ♩ = 74

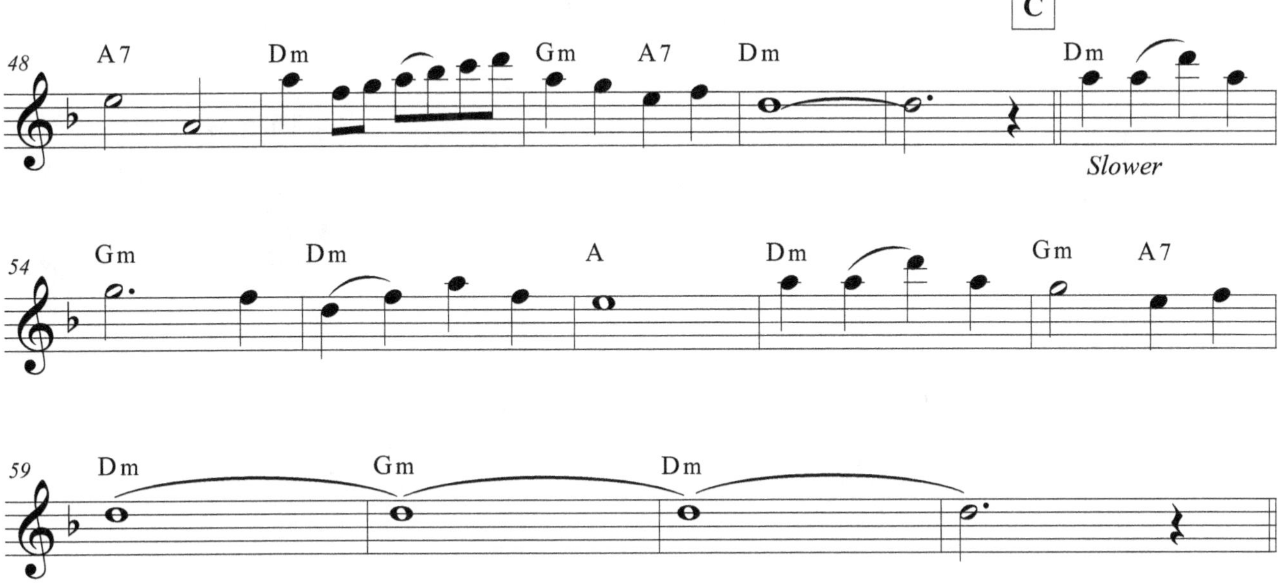
C
48
A7
Dm
Gm
A7
Dm
Dm
Slower
54
Gm
Dm
A
Dm
Gm
A7
59
Dm
Gm
Dm

Lo! He Comes, with Clouds Descending
Helmsley

Strum Guitar Acc.

Thomas Augustine Arne
arr. by William Bay

Boldly ♩ = 132

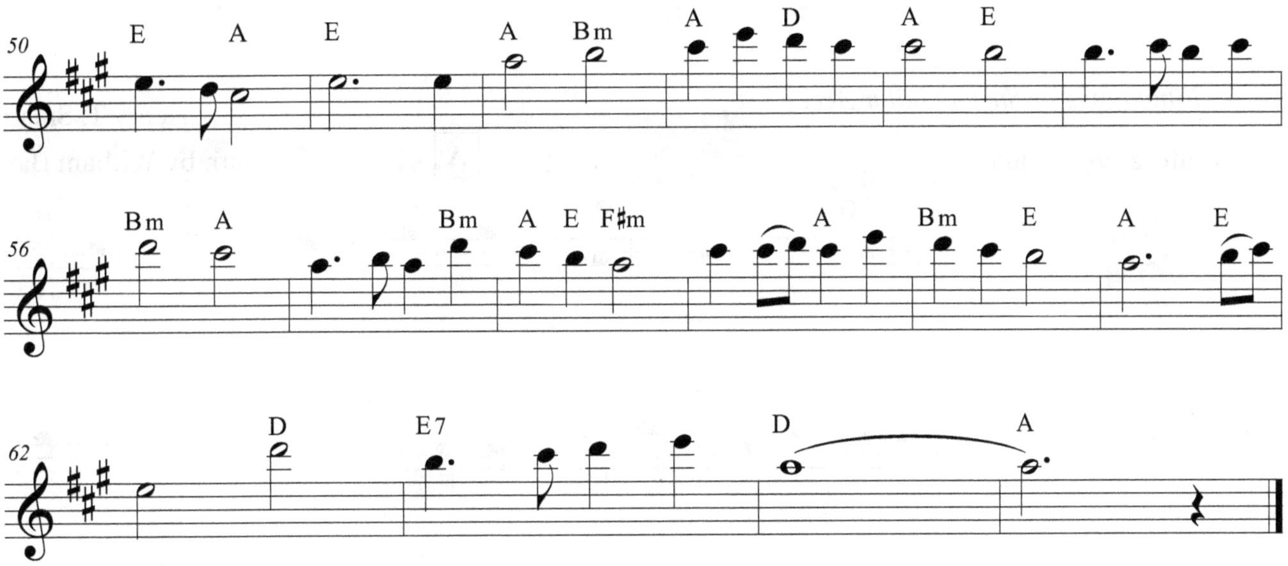
50
E A E A Bm A D A E
56
Bm A Bm A E F♯m A Bm E A E
62
D E7 D A

Lead On, O King Eternal
Lancashire

Fingerstyle or Strum Guitar Acc.

Henry T. Smart
arr. by William Bay

Moderately ♩ = 106

Lord, Speak to Me
Canonbury

Fingerstyle Guitar Acc.

Robert Schumann
arr. by William Bay

Lyrically ♩ = 90

Love Divine
Beecher

Fingerstyle Guitar Acc.

John Zundel
arr. by William Bay

Moderato ♩ = 100

My Hope is Built on Nothing Less
Solid Rock

Guitar: Capo 3rd Fret and Play Chords in Parentheses

William Bradbury
arr. by William Bay

Fingerstyle or Strum Guitar Acc.

Moderato ♩ = 106

My Jesus, I Love Thee
Gordon

Fingerstyle Guitar Acc.

Adoniram J. Gordon

arr. by William Bay

Now Thank We All Our God
Nun Danket

Strum or Fingerstyle Guitar Acc.

Johan Crüger
arr. by William Bay

O God, We Praise Thee
Morning Song

Fingerstyle Guitar Acc.

Anonymous
Wyeth's Repository of Sacred Music, 1813

Gently ♩ = 82

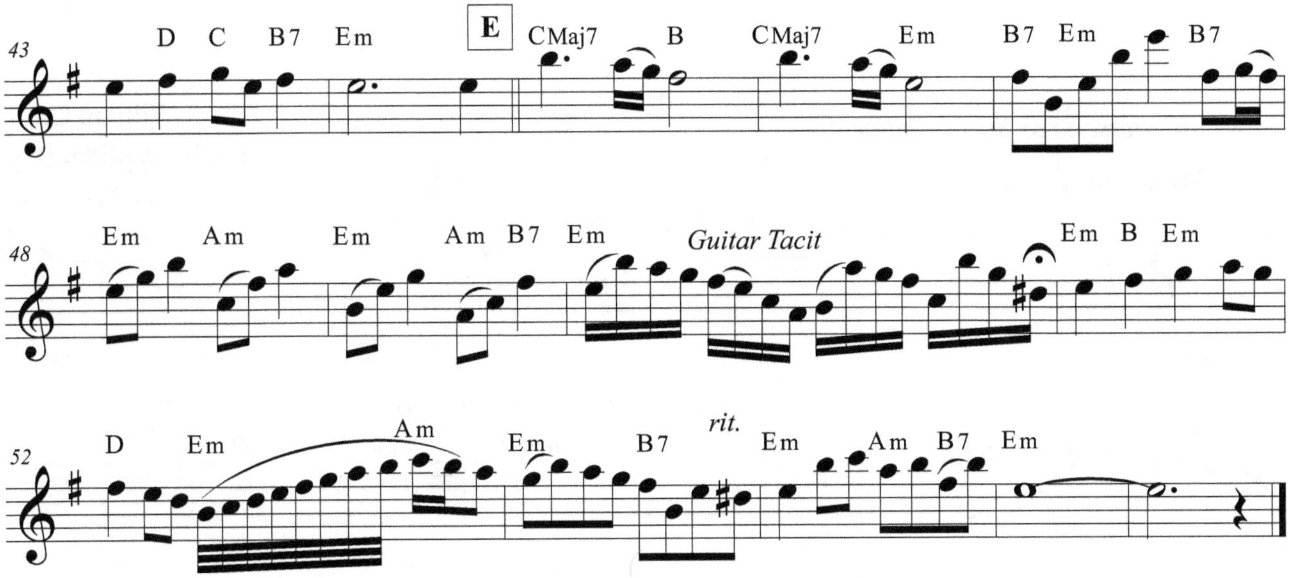
43
D C B7 Em
E
CMaj7 B CMaj7 Em B7 Em B7
48
Em Am Em Am B7 Em
Guitar Tacit
Em B Em
52
D Em Am Em B7
rit.
Em Am B7 Em

O God, Our Help in Ages Past
St. Anne

William Croft
arr. by William Bay

Fingerstyle or Strum Guitar Acc

O Master, Let Me Walk with Thee
Maryton

Fingerstyle Guitar Acc.

H. Percy Smith

arr. by William Bay

Andante ♩ = 100

O Praise Ye the Lord!
Laudate Dominum

Fingerstyle or Strum Guitar Acc.

Charles Hubert Hastings Parry

arr. by William Bay

O Sacred Head, Now Wounded
Herzlich Tut Mich Verlangen

Fingerstyle Guitar Accompaniment

J.S. Bach
arr. by William Bay

O Savior, Rend the Heavens Wide
O Heiland, Reiss Die Himmel Auf

Strum Guitar Acc.

Boldly ♩ = 100

Gesanbuch, Augsburg, 1666

arr. by William Bay

O Worship the King
Lyons

Fingerstyle or Strum Guitar Acc.

Johann Michael Haydn

arr. by William Bay

Boldly ♩ = 112

Oh, For a Thousand Tongues to Sing
Azmon

Strum Guitar Acc.

Moderato ♩ = 112

A

Lowell Mason
arr. by William Bay

Oh, the Deep, Deep Love of Jesus
Ebenezer

Fingerstyle or Strum Guitar Acc.

Thomas J. Williams
arr. by William Bay

Moderato ♩ = 100

Praise My Soul, the King of Heaven
Lauda Anima

Fingerstyle or Strum Guitar Acc.

John Goss, 1869

arr. by William Bay

Boldly ♩ = 96

49
G7 Am C Dm G D7
55
G G7 D D7 G Am G F C
61
Am Dm G F C Dm C G7 C
C
C F G C F C
rit.
72
Dm G7 Am G7 C

Praise to the Lord, the Almighty
Lobe den Herren

Strum Guitar Acc.

Joachim Neander

arr. by William Bay

Boldly ♩ = 110

Rejoice, O Pure in Heart
Marion

Guitar: Capo 3rd Fret and Play Chords in Parentheses

Arthur H. Messiter

arr. by William Bay

Rejoice, the Lord is King
Darwall

Shall We Gather at the River/Alternate Melody
Palmetto

Fingerstyle Guitar Acc.

Early American Hymn

arr. by William Bay

Adagio ♩ = 66

Sing Praise to God Who Reigns Above
Mit Freuden Zart

Fingerstyle Guitar Acc.

Bohemian Brethren's Kirchengesänge

arr. by William Bay

Moderato ♩ = 98

Spirit of God, Descend upon My Heart
Morecambe

Fingerstyle Guitar Acc.

Frederick C. Atkinson
arr. by William Bay

Lyrically ♩ = 98

Thaxted
Sung as "O God Beyond All Praising"

Fingerstyle or Strum Guitar Acc.

Gustav Holst/From "The Planets"

arr. by William Bay

Boldly ♩ = 96

54
A F♯m E A C♯m F♯m D E F♯m E
59
D E A C♯m D E F♯m A D E
C
Slower
rit.
64
A C♯m D E F♯m D A C♯m D A

Star of the County Down
Sung As "The Mighty God with Power Speaks"

Fingerstyle Guitar Acc.

Traditional Irish
arr. by William Bay

Lyrically ♩ = 92

104

The Church's One Foundation
Aurelia

Fingerstyle Guitar Acc.

Samuel Wesley
arr. by William Bay

The God of Abraham Praise
Leoni

Meyer Lyon
arr. by William Bay

Fingerstyle Guitar Acc.

Moderately ♩ = 108

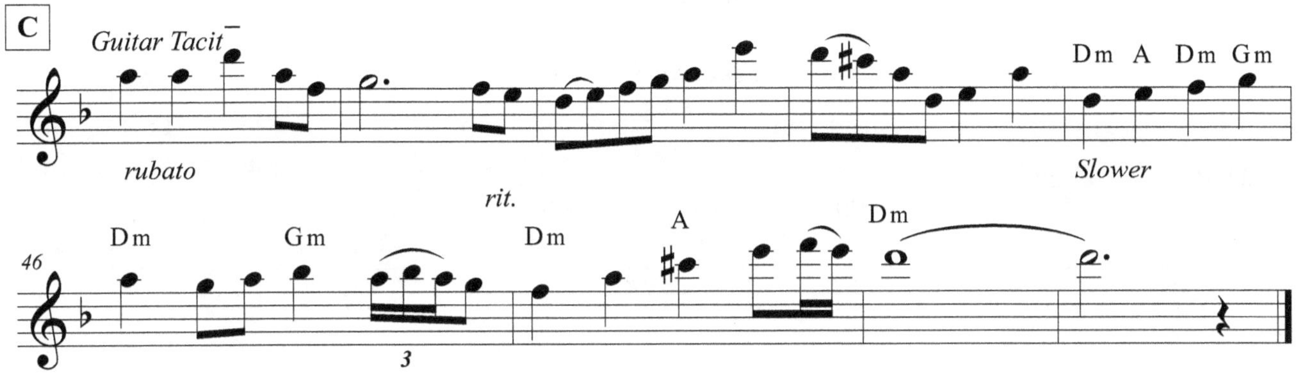
C
Guitar Tacit
rubato
Dm A Dm Gm
Slower
rit.
46
Dm
Gm
3
Dm
A
Dm

The Day is Past and Gone
Evening Shade

Guitar: Capo 3rd Fret and Play Chords in Parentheses

Anonynous
Sacred Harp, 1835
arr. by William Bay

The King of Love My Shepherd Is
St. Columba

Fingerstyle Guitar Acc.

Traditional Irish
arr. by William Bay

Lyrically ♩ = 90

The Lord is My Shepherd
Brother James' Air

Guitar: Capo 1st Fret and Play Chords in Parentheses

Fingerstyle or Strum Guitar Acc.

J. L. Macbeth Bain

arr. by William Bay

Gently ♩ = 94

The Lord Our God is Clothed with Might
Detroit

Fingerstyle Guitar Acc.

Moderately ♩ = 102

Kentucky Harmony, 1820
arr. by William Bay

The Lord's Supper
Way

Fingerstyle Guitar Acc.

William Bay

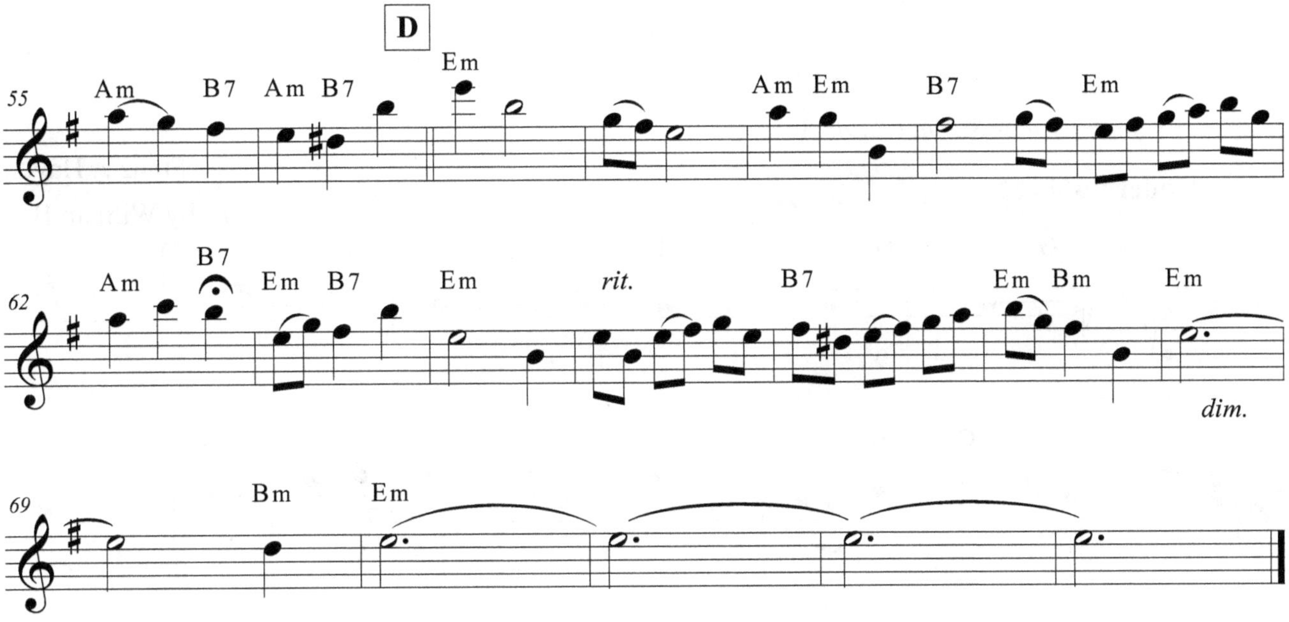
D
55
Am B7 Am B7 Em Am Em B7 Em
62
Am B7 Em B7 Em rit. B7 Em Bm Em
dim.
69
Bm Em

The Spacious Firmament on High
Creation

Franz J. Haydn
arr. by William Bay

Fingerstyle or Strum Guitar Acc.

51
Bm A E7 A E A E A D A E
57
E7 Bm A E7 A E A
63
E A E A E A E
69
A E A E A Bm
More Slowly
75
A E7 A E A Bm A E7 A

The Lord's My Shepherd
Crimond

Fingerstyle Guitar Acc.

Jessie Seymour Irvine

arr. by William Bay

Moderately ♩ = 92

The Strife is O'er, the Battle Done
Victory

Strum or Fingerstyle Guitar Acc.

Giovanni de Palestrina, 1591
arr. by William Bay

Boldly ♩ = 134

The Wedding Feast of Cana
Ag an bPósadh Bhi i gCána

Traditional Irish
arr. by William Bay

Fingerstyle or Strum Guitar Acc.

This is My Father's World
Terra Beata

Fingerstyle Guitar Acc.

Franklin L. Sheppard

arr. by William Bay

Moderato ♩ = 98

119

Thine is the Glory
Judas Maccabaeus

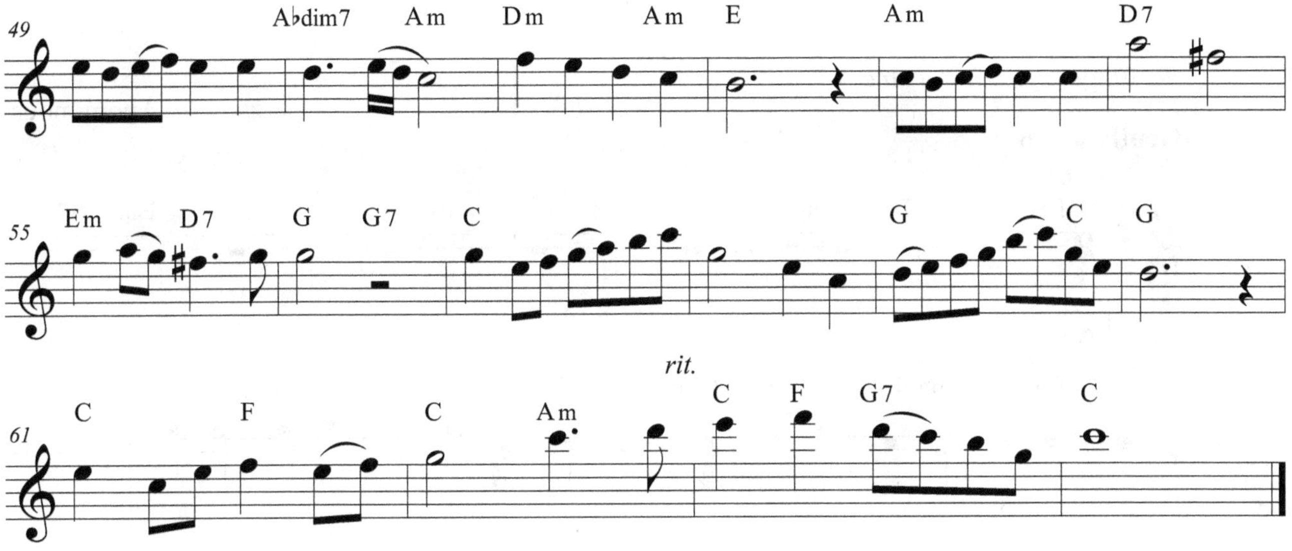
49
A♭dim7 Am Dm Am E Am D7
55
Em D7 G G7 C G C G
rit.
61
C F C Am C F G7 C

Veni Redemptor gentium
Plainsong, 12th Century

Fingerstyle Guitar Acc

Anonymous
arr. by William Bay

Gently ♩ = 86

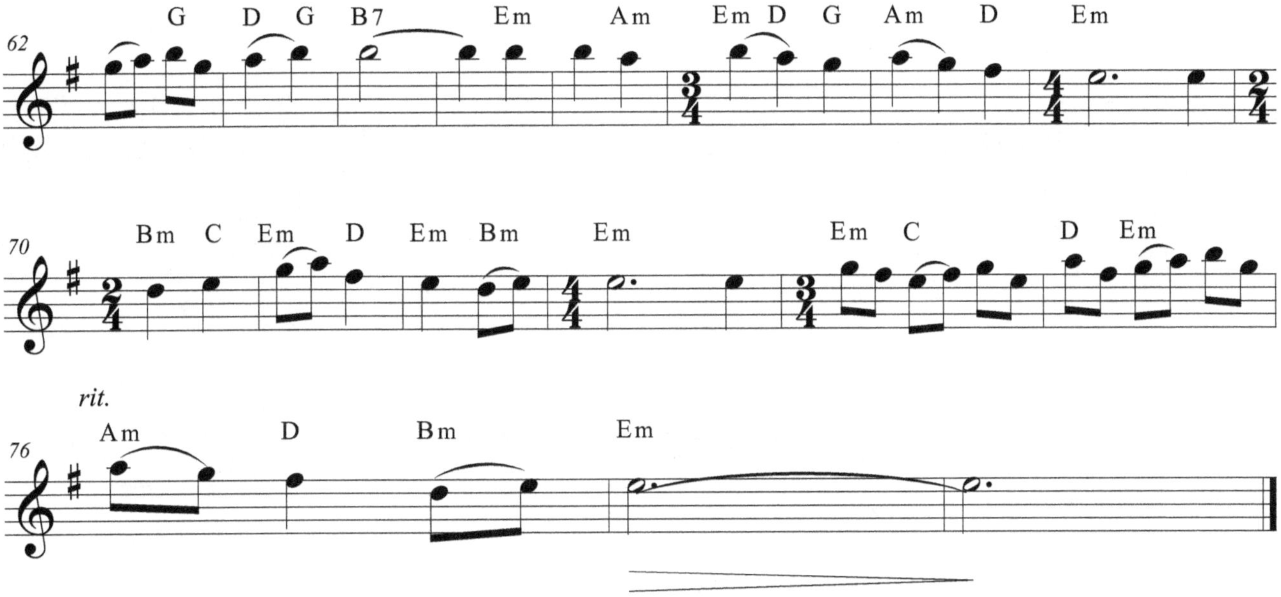
62
G D G B7 Em Am Em D G Am D Em
70
Bm C Em D Em Bm Em Em C D Em
rit.
76
Am D Bm Em

Watchman, Tell Us of the Night
Aberystwyth

Fingerstyle Guitar Acc.

Joseph Parry
arr. by William Bay

Moderately ♩ = 96

Wayfarin' Stranger

Fingerstyle or Strum Guitar Acc.

Traditional Spiritual
arr. by William Bay

We Gather Together
Kremser

Fingerstyle Guitar Acc.

Nederlandtsch Gedenckclank, 1626
arr. by William Bay

Lyrically ♩ = 98

Were You There?

Fingerstyle Guitar Acc.

Traditional Spiritual
arr. by William Bay

Andante ♩ = 74

When Jesus Left His Father's Throne
Kingsfold

Fingerstlyle or Strum Guitar Acc.

Traditional English
arr. by William Bay

Majestically ♩ = 104

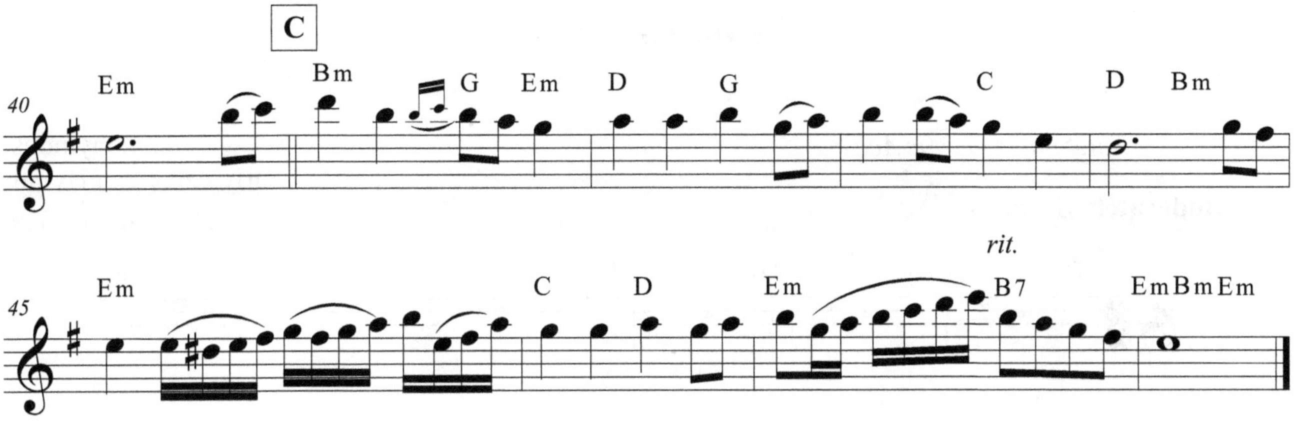
C
40
Em
Bm
G
Em
D
G
C
D
Bm
rit.
45
Em
C
D
Em
B7
Em Bm Em

What Wondrous Love
Wondrous Love

Fingerstyle Guitar Acc.

Anonymous
Early American Hymn
arr. by William Bay

Moderately ♩ = 96

50
FMaj7 Em Dm Am G Am F Dm F Em
3
C
55
G C F Em Am G Am
60
G Em Am Dm FMaj7 Em G Am
65
G Am Em F Am FMaj7 Am

When I Survey the Wondrous Cross
Rockingham

Fingerstlyle or Strum Guitar Acc.

Isaac Watts
arr. by William Bay

Moderately ♩ = 110